DYNAMIC PRAYER

DYNAMIC PRAYER

COMMUNICATING WITH GOD

DAVID NOAKES

Sovereign World

Published by Sovereign World Ltd
PO Box 784
Ellel
Lancaster
LA1 9DA
United Kingdom

www.sovereignworld.com

ISBN: 978 1 85240 625 7

The publishers aim to produce books which will help to extend and build up the
Kingdom of God. We do not necessarily agree with every view expressed by the
authors, or with every interpretation of Scripture expressed. We expect readers to
make their own judgment in the light of their understanding of God's Word and
in an attitude of Christian love and fellowship.

Printed in the United Kingdom

CONTENTS

CHAPTER I

BASIC PRINCIPLES

In recent years, the words of Scripture in 2 Chronicles 7:14 have become very familiar: "if my people, who are called by my name, will humble themselves and pray and seek my face and turn from their wicked ways, then will I hear from heaven and will forgive their sin and will heal their land."

The situation which confronts us as the people of God is one of great urgency. In the words of Hosea 10:12, "it is time to seek the LORD, until he comes and showers righteousness on you" and the condition in which we must come before the Lord has already been spelt out in the same verse: "Sow for yourselves righteousness, reap the fruit of unfailing love, and break up your unploughed ground". It is a spiritual law that if we desire to reap the fruit of righteousness in our situation, we must first sow righteousness in our own lives.

If our eyes are open to see the state of sickness in our own nation as it truly is, and if our spirits have been touched with an awareness of the grief of God over our national condition and of the judgment which we must surely bring upon ourselves if there is no repentance, then our hearts should be crying out to God for His remedy for such sickness.

We need the healing touch of God upon our land. The nations of the world are desperately sick, both spiritually and morally, as a result of the people having turned their backs upon God and substituted the worship of false gods. In the West it is the gods of materialism and of secular humanism that are dominant, and in recent years we have opened the door to the spiritual forces of anarchy as a result of passing laws which are contrary to the Word of God. What God calls sin, we have declared lawful, but the Word of God does not change to suit human whims or culture. 1 John 3:4 declares that "sin is lawlessness", and in our blindness and ignorance we have to face the fact that we are indeed reaping what we ourselves have sown.

WHAT IS THE SOLUTION?

Yet all of this has been taking place during the same period of time during which the Charismatic Renewal movement has been powerfully active in the church. This movement, of which so much was hoped for so long, has apparently had no significant impact on the condition of the Western nations. We have enjoyed the renewing effect of the Holy Spirit's activity; we have been glad to receive the renewed manifestations of the spiritual gifts; we have been blessed by the outpouring of new songs and by revitalised worship. Yet there it has often ended. Why have greater things not come to pass? Why has revival not come upon the church? Why are the nations still gripped with sickness, and continuing to deteriorate so alarmingly?

We have failed to understand that God does not change His ways. The answer lies in those words of 2 Chronicles 7:14 quoted at the beginning of this chapter. If we truly desire God to "hear from heaven, forgive our sin and heal our land", then we must take serious heed to the conditions upon which He will do so. They are fourfold: we, the people of God, must

1. humble ourselves
2. pray
3. seek the face of God, and
4. repent of our own wicked ways.

The unhappy truth is that on the whole, during the period of the Charismatic Renewal movement, these aspects of our calling as Christians have found little popularity, and have indeed in many places hardly been mentioned in our congregations. Yet they are vital because revival will not come unless amongst us there has first been a humbling which admits our total helplessness to accomplish any deep spiritual work by our own efforts and devices. The Holy Spirit is calling for earnest persevering prayer and a seeking of the face of God for His own sake rather than for what we hope to obtain from Him, together with honest repentance in areas where our lives, both individual and corporate, have failed to measure up to the plumb line test of the Word of God.

God is seeking a people of holiness who will walk in His ways; a people of obedience who will walk in the fear of the Lord, taking His Word seriously and obeying it; a people of commitment who will face the awful reality of the situation in both church and nation, and will undertake the task of tackling it in the ways of God, by persevering intercessory prayer.

A prophecy given in 1906 during the Azusa Street revival in Los Angeles said that in the last days of the Pentecostal movement "there will be an overemphasis on praise to a God they no longer pray to." We can often be tempted towards substitutes for prayer, but God never departs from His own ways.

The situation is one of warfare. The enemy is coming in "like a flood", but in response "the Spirit of the LORD shall lift up a standard against him" (Isaiah 59:19 KJV), and God is seeking from among His people a Gideon's army to wield the spiritual weapons of warfare, obedient to His commands, alert and responsive to His revealed strategy and timing. That army of the Lord will contain a large body of those who are committed to intercessory prayer.

WHAT IS INTERCESSION?

The word used in Hebrew, *paga*, has connotations of an activity that seeks to exercise strong influence and persuasion. In Jeremiah 27:18 it is rendered as pleading with God, while in 36:25 we find men urging the king not to burn Jeremiah's scroll. This word implies an activity in prayer which causes a response in the heart of God as a result of which He meets with those who are the object of that prayer. In Isaiah 53:12 we find that Jesus "made intercession for the transgressors", pleading with the Father on behalf of sinners on the basis of the fact that He had borne our sins and made atonement by the shedding of His own blood.

When we come to the Greek of the New Testament, the word used is *entugchano*, which has the meaning of meeting with and of coming between, and is used four times, in Romans 8:27, 8:34 and 11:2 and in Hebrews 7:25. On one occasion in Romans 8:26 the word *huper-entugchano* is used, giving additional emphasis to the fact that the prayer is a meeting with God specifically on behalf of another:

Intercession is a totally selfless form of prayer, seeking God not on behalf of the one who is praying, but on behalf of another person or situation which needs to be affected by the grace and power of the Lord. It is motivated by love for God and for those concerned, and it urges God to do something about the situation.

It is supremely the form of prayer which moves the hand of God in power to do what human beings cannot accomplish by their own efforts.

In Ezekiel 22 God tells the prophet, who is already in exile in Babylon, of the state of sin in the city of Jerusalem. Following a devastating account of how God sees the situation, we then find Him saying to Ezekiel in verse 30, "I looked for a man among them who would build up the wall and stand before me in the gap on behalf of the land so that I would not have to destroy it, but I found none."

In this scripture we have a classic description of what the intercessor is called to do. He "stands in the gap" as a link between God and the situation which is disordered and which needs to be set right by the Lord's activity, or which is threatened with judgment and needs to receive God's mercy rather than His anger. The intercessor's activity is that of pleading with a superior on behalf of an inferior, just as an advocate in court will plead with the judge on behalf of his or her client.

A DIVINE ACTIVITY AND A PRIESTLY ACTIVITY

The importance of intercession in the purposes of God is underlined by the fact that it is in itself a divine activity. We read in Isaiah 53:12 that Jesus "made intercession for the transgressors" and in Hebrews 7:25 that "he is able to save completely those who come to God through him, because he always lives to intercede for them", while in Romans 8:26–27 we are told that the Holy Spirit "intercedes for us with groans that words cannot express" and that "the Spirit intercedes for the saints in accordance with God's will."

Intercession is also a priestly activity. We have just seen from Hebrews 7:25 that Jesus always lives to intercede for His people, and this statement is set in the context of the fact that He is a permanent high priest. Under the Old Covenant it was the high priest who entered the Holy of Holies in the Temple on the Day of Atonement, representing the whole nation of Israel before the Lord, and offering sprinkled blood as an atonement, or covering, for the sins of the people (Leviticus 16:11–17).

In Old Testament times there were two principal types of religious leader in Israel: the prophet and the priest. Their two functions were opposite and complementary; the prophet represented God to the people and acted as His spokesman, while the priest represented the people before God and pleaded with Him on their behalf. The priestly role was therefore that of an intercessor, standing in the gap between God and human beings.

In 1 Peter 2:9 we learn that as the Body of Christ we are corporately a "royal priesthood", and we should function as a priestly people because together we are the Body of Jesus, the Great High Priest. In this context one of our corporate responsibilities is that of intercession; but sadly it is an area in which we often fail disastrously. We seem to have lost all idea of the effectiveness of corporate prayer, and we need a fresh awareness of the power of God's activity which would be released if we obeyed the command in 1 Timothy 2:1–8, where in verses 1 and 2 we are urged "that requests, prayers, intercession and thanksgiving be made for everyone – for kings and all those in authority".

The early church devoted themselves, we learn in Acts 2:42, to four principal areas of activity in their times of assembling together – teaching, fellowship, breaking of bread and prayer. Yet in our day, it is possible to go to meeting after meeting in fellowships of all types and find no corporate prayer. In this matter, we are being disobedient to the Word of God, and we are depriving both the church and the nation of blessings which would result if we were to repent and restore corporate intercession to our gatherings. Our failure in this area is something which needs to be seriously considered by leaders in every local church because we shall be called to account if we do not lead the flock of God in the ways of His appointing.

QUESTIONS

1. There is a scriptural principle that we reap what we sow. How can you see this to be true at a national level?
2. What can we do to hasten spiritual revival?
3. How does intercession differ from other forms of prayer? What does God require of us corporately, and how should we go about it?
4. In what ways should we act as a "royal priesthood"?

CHAPTER 2

WHY IS INTERCESSION NECESSARY?

We sometimes wonder: if God is all-wise and all-powerful, why should He need help from anybody? If He always knows exactly what needs to be done, why should He wait for human beings to cooperate with Him? Why doesn't He just get on and do what needs to be done? Why does He bother Himself by getting us involved in the working of His kingdom and His creation? Why does He call on us to intercede? Couldn't He manage perfectly well without prayer? The obvious answer is: yes, of course, God can manage perfectly well without us. Why then does He choose not to do so?

Fundamental to all God's dealings with His people is the concept of relationship. This is built into the very heart of the nature of the triune God – three persons, unique and distinct, with differing functions: the Father, planning what is to happen, the Son, who gives form and utterance to these purposes, and the Holy Spirit, who executes them in practice. Yet the three persons of God act together in perfect harmony and cooperation, no one of them acting against or independently of the others. The Father loves the Son and shows Him all He does, while Jesus does only what He sees the Father doing (John 5:19–20), and the Holy Spirit speaks only what He hears from the Father and the Son (John 16:13–15).

The concept of relationship is a vital key to understanding the purposes of God's heart and the ways in which He acts. The people of Israel could see the mighty deeds of God, but it was only those who, like Moses, had received the Holy Spirit to empower them for ministry, who could receive revelation and understanding of God's ways (Psalm 103:7).

Now, however, the Holy Spirit is freely available to all believers, and our Father wants us to enter increasingly into a spirit-to-spirit, heart-to-heart walk with Him which the work of the Holy Spirit makes possible as He enlarges our understanding and reveals to us more of the nature and ways of God.

This is how God wants it to be between Himself and His people. Even under the Old Covenant, before the Spirit had been freely given to all God's people, God saw His relationship with Israel as that of a husband to a bride; He was jealous of that relationship, and grieved deeply at Israel's unfaithfulness in turning away from Him into idolatry, which He viewed as spiritual adultery and prostitution. This was so serious to God that a man like Hosea was even commanded to marry a prostitute so that he could convey to God's people exactly how God felt about their breach of covenant relationship (Hosea 1:2–3).

It is not until we understand how the heart of God feels on any given issue that we begin to understand why He acts as He does. The account of creation in Genesis tells us that the Lord created Adam for mutual fellowship and enjoyed meeting with Him in the garden. The Fall brought loss not only to Adam; God also was deprived of the joy of fellowship, because sin put up a barrier between Him and Adam (Isaiah 59:2). It was the Lord's continuing desire for close relationship and faithful fellowship which has since led first to the creation of Israel as a special nation and subsequently to the creation of the church. When finally all the things of this age have passed away and the new heaven and the new earth described in Revelation 21 and 22 have come into being, the one and only survivor of this age will be the Bride of Christ. The creation and preparation of the Bride is God's ultimate purpose in human history, and the motivating factor lies in the very nature of the heart of God, and the love which longs for a perfect relationship of mutual love and trust.

When we understand this, we begin to be able to realise why it is that the Lord has chosen to work only in cooperation with His people. Yes, of course He can manage alone and indeed, Isaiah 59:16 and 63:5 make it plain that He will indeed do so if there is no one to act with Him – but this is not the way of His choosing.

A PATHWAY TO MATURITY

God has revealed His nature as that of a father. He is a father who longs to bring His children to maturity, and children do not develop and mature in a home where the parents will never permit them to be involved in their activities for fear that they will make a mess of what is going on.

Like a good parent, our heavenly Father chooses to involve us as far as possible in what He is doing as "God's fellow-workers" (1 Corinthians 3:9), overruling our errors and even weaving them into the outworking of His purposes. We learn from both successes and mistakes, and we are brought to maturity by the working in our lives of the Holy Spirit's teaching of the Word to us and the experience of being led by Him in practical application of the ways of God.

In no area of experience do we learn faster than in the place of real prayer. It is there that God reveals to us the secrets of His heart. It is in the place of intercession over situations of difficulty that we learn how God thinks. It is as we seek Him for understanding of how we should pray that we begin to receive revelation of the wisdom of God, who knows how to deal with every situation, and as often as not in ways of which we ourselves would never have thought. It is as we seek Him at times when we are caught up in the spiritual battle which rages around us that we learn His ways of overcoming the forces of evil. There is no activity which provides a quicker route to spiritual maturity than that of intercession. It is a training ground where God transforms ignorant children into seasoned warriors who can form part of a Bride equipped to share the throne of the Lord Jesus Christ and to be a fit partner for Him.

AN EXPRESSION OF GOD'S MERCY

There are other reasons why we are called to intercession. Our common inheritance of Adam's sinful nature has created a barrier between God and humanity. For believers in the Lord Jesus Christ, the barrier has been torn down and we each have free access through His blood into the very presence of the Father (Hebrews 10:19–22). Yet the love and compassion of God is towards all people, saved and unsaved alike (John 3:16–17). He "wants all men to be saved" (1 Timothy 2:4), but there is a barrier between Him and them. He desires to influence and direct the affairs of both individuals and nations for their good and in order to save from disaster, but most of those who govern the nations do not know Him. He sees sin which cries out for righteous judgment, but although He longs to have mercy, those in danger do not know who or where He is, so they do not know to whom they should turn.

In all these situations there is a gap between God and humanity, and God looks as He did in Jerusalem (Ezekiel 22:30) for someone who is able to stand in that gap and plead with Him over the situation so that He may be persuaded to do what in His love and mercy He longs to do, and to withhold the judgment which the laws of justice and righteousness would otherwise require.

The great intercessors of Scripture understood this principle, and give us an example to follow. In Genesis 18:16–33 we encounter Abraham in the activity of standing in the gap. The account is both revealing and yet tantalising in its outcome. First, in verses 17 to 19 we learn of the Lord's desire to tell Abraham about what He was intending to do to the evil city of Sodom, because He wanted this man in covenant-relationship with Him to share in what He was doing.

Abraham's response was to stand in the gap and plead with God for the inhabitants of Sodom. From a personal and purely human point of view, there seems to have been little reason why Abraham should have cared greatly about the fate of Sodom, apart from the fact that his nephew Lot lived there. Yet he was sensitive to what the Spirit of God was really wanting of him, and he began to plead with the Lord that the whole of Sodom should be spared for the sake of those in it who were righteous.

Abraham teaches us a lesson in perseverance, for he besought the Lord six times on the matter, not resting from his prayers until the Lord had agreed to spare Sodom if even only ten righteous people were to be found there, but it is at this point that the story becomes tantalizing.

Sodom contained fewer than ten righteous people and the Lord did destroy it! Would God have spared the city if Abraham had persevered even further? The Scripture is silent on the matter – but Abraham's intercession on behalf of the righteous was nevertheless effective. Although destruction came upon Sodom, God rescued Lot, the only righteous man in the city, and his wife and daughters.

Psalm 106 gives a detailed account of the sins of the people of Israel following their deliverance out of Egypt. From verse 19 onwards comes a reference to the making and worshipping of a golden calf at Horeb, and in verse 23 God "said he would destroy them – had not Moses, his chosen one, stood in the breach before him to keep his wrath from destroying them." Here again we see a man of God interceding on behalf of those who would otherwise have suffered God's overwhelming judgment upon their sin. Moses "stood in the breach before him" pleading on behalf of the people. We see also the grace of God in the heart of the intercessor, for in the account in Exodus 32 we find first that Moses interceded successfully for the people (vv. 9–14) and then in verses 30 to 32 he is found even offering his own life as atonement for their sin.

To us, it seems entirely predictable that the Lord did not accept this offer, because we now know what Moses presumably did not, that only the totally sinless blood of Christ, the lamb without blemish, is adequate as atonement for sin; but we have to marvel at the love of God in the heart of Moses for the sinful people for whom he was interceding. The people were not at all easy to lead; they grumbled, they rebelled, they murmured against Moses, they had even threatened to stone him. Yet despite all, when God offered (vv. 9–10) to destroy them all, and make a new great nation out of Moses' descendants alone, the heart of the intercessor not only discerned the Lord's underlying desire to forgive the people and pleaded successfully on their behalf, but was even willing to offer himself for punishment in their place.

God's covenant would not have failed if He had done as He had offered, for any descendants of Moses would still have been the seed of Abraham, Isaac and Jacob (although it would have been true that much of Jacob's prophecy in Genesis 49 would have remained unfulfilled). The temptation for Moses to accept must have been very great, and it can only have been his love for God and for his brethren, and his intimate knowledge of the heart of God which caused him to adopt the course of the sacrificial intercessor. His action of selfless love saved an entire nation from destruction.

To conclude this chapter, we should note also that the prophet Samuel, in the midst of a demonstration of God's displeasure with a rebellious people, stated that he would not fail to pray for them, because to do so would be for him to sin against the Lord (1 Samuel 12:19–23). For the man of God, intercession on behalf of the people of God was a sacred duty and an act of obedience.

QUESTIONS

1. Why does God want His people to pray?
2. Why is it important to understand God's ways?
3. God is not content for us to remain "babes in Christ". In what ways does He bring us to maturity?
4. What do the examples of Abraham, Moses and Samuel teach us about the character of a mature intercessor?

CHAPTER 3

WHO SHOULD INTERCEDE?

The basic qualification for carrying out the task of intercession is that of being in covenant-relationship with God. Although the Lord has compassion and will often hear and respond to those who are not in such a relationship when they cry out to Him in earnest, nevertheless it is only those who are within the bonds of the covenant with God who are able to come before His face and prevail on behalf of others.

Under the Old Covenant, even this privilege had limitations, for it was only the high priest who could enter the Holy of Holies, and then only once a year on the Day of Atonement. Intimate relationship with God was reserved for a very few, and the privilege was rare. Abraham was known as "the Friend of God" (James 2:23 KJV), and we have already noted how God chose to reveal to him His purposes concerning Sodom, an example of the principle that "the Sovereign LORD does nothing without revealing his plan to his servants the prophets" (Amos 3:7).

Moses was a "chosen one" (Psalm 106:23), a man "whom the

LORD knew face to face" (Deuteronomy 34:10). God spoke directly to David and to Solomon, and gave great revelation to men such as Joseph and Daniel, while the prophets all had the Holy Spirit's anointing upon them for the task of ministry, and received the revelation of God directly by word or in vision, or both.

Throughout the time of the Old Testament it was men such as these, enabled by the Holy Spirit, who are recorded as interceding on behalf of the people and prevailing with God. Under the New Covenant, however, all believers have direct access to the very presence of God through the blood of Jesus, and receive the gift of the Holy Spirit both to dwell within them for salvation and to empower them for the ministry or service to which they are called. All Christians are therefore potentially effective intercessors.

THE LORD CALLS WHOM HE CHOOSES

Beyond this, however, it is unquestionably the case that for some Christians the Lord gives a calling to a much deeper commitment to intercessory prayer. This work of service to the Lord and to the whole Body of Christ is foundational to the effective functioning of all other ministries, and also plays a vital role in the protection of those who are called to function in them. The apostle, prophet, evangelist, pastor or teacher who lack those who will intercede and bear them up continually before the throne of grace are in a lonely and vulnerable position indeed.

The calling to a committed ministry of intercession brings both a high privilege and a heavy burden. It requires a sharing of the heart of God concerning people and situations. Sometimes intercessors will rejoice with God, but more often they will weep and travail with Him as His co-workers, as was the case with a man such as Nehemiah (Nehemiah 1:4). Sometimes they will fast and labour in prayer over long periods of time, even to the point of exhaustion. Most of their labour will be done in the secret place where there is no glamour, no approval from others; yet despite this they are sharing in the front line of spiritual warfare, and what they do is so vital to the fulfilment of God's purposes that they are often subject to the attacks of Satan, who delights to hinder them or, if possible, to cause them to give up altogether.

Yet this is also a ministry which brings its own rewards – the reward of a close and intimate walk with God, the reward of sharing in His joy when His will is seen to be prevailing, the reward of knowing that this work of service is crucial to the right functioning of the Body of Christ, the reward of hearing the words "Well done, thou good and faithful servant" (Matthew 25:21 KJV) from a faithful Father who never fails to see and reward what is done in the secret place of prayer (Matthew 6:6). Such men and women are vital warriors in the church at such a time as this, when the enemy is indeed coming in like a flood.

SHOULD INTERCESSION BE CARRIED OUT ALONE OR CORPORATELY?
The answer is both. It is often the case that when you are alone, you will experience a sudden urging from the Holy Spirit to begin praying concerning some particular matter, and when that urging comes it usually indicates the need for an immediate response. If the burden is very great, you may find it necessary to put down all that you are doing, or even to postpone other arrangements, in order to devote yourself entirely to answering the Holy Spirit's call and standing in a gap where you are urgently needed.

This is not at all unusual and at such times you will be perfectly able to prevail in prayer alone, for "The prayer of (one) righteous man is powerful and effective" (James 5:16). Elijah's prayers were totally effective, even though he was alone in praying them.

Nevertheless, there is another principle stated in Scripture which is significant for us. In Ecclesiastes 4:9–12, we read that "Two are better than one, because they have a good return for their work: If one falls down, his friend can help him up. But pity the man who falls and has no-one to help him up ... Though one may be overpowered, two can defend themselves. A cord of three strands is not quickly broken."

We have already noted that the work of intercession is a target for attack by the forces of Satan. Prevailing prayer poses a bigger threat to his kingdom than any other activity we can undertake, so what could be more logical than to attempt to hinder or totally prevent the activity of the intercessor? The devil seeks to "wear out the saints of the most High" (Daniel 7:25 KJV) and has many strategies. He may bring weariness or heaviness; he may seek to distract the mind by preoccupying it with matters of concern in your own life; he may remind you of things which you have not done, which suddenly seem to be of vital urgency (although they would not have been, half an hour earlier!). The doorbell or the telephone may ring, usually for some trivial reason; the baby may start crying; the dog suddenly deposits its last meal on the sitting-room carpet – the possibilities are almost endless!

This sort of thing is no accident, but a policy of deliberate hindrance and harassment. Alone, you can be totally overwhelmed. If you do have to enter into times of intercession alone, be deliberate in asking the Lord to protect you and your time from the activities of the evil one. Take the whole armour of God, plead the effectiveness of the blood of Jesus against the workings of the kingdom of darkness, and request the Lord to surround you with the protection of His angels – that is one of their functions (Hebrews 1:14).

If possible, however, it is best when interceding on a regular basis to join together with at least one other warrior. There is great strength and blessing when two or more saints come before the Lord together. If one is feeling oppressed, the other can bring relief. If one is getting tired, the other can take up the burden. While one is praying, the other can be not only agreeing but also listening for the promptings of the Holy Spirit to bring needed revelation or further direction as to how to pray.

What is an ideal number? Too many can lead to confusion and to a lack of cohesiveness of vision concerning the task in hand. Experience suggests that two or three, or even four, can make a good intercessory unit, provided that there is a real unity in spirit between those who are involved. Any major area of disagreement can prove a great hindrance, even if attempts are being made to sweep it under the carpet; somebody is going to stumble over it sooner or later. "Can two walk together, except they be agreed?" says Amos 3:3 (KJV). Unity and mutual trust are essential.

There is also the activity of corporate intercession by the whole assembly of God's people in one place. Wisely and firmly led, under the direction of the Holy Spirit, there is great potential power in such prayer. There is an urgent need for the restoration of corporate intercession on a regular basis in every local church assembly, and we should not be deterred by the fear of making mistakes or getting into confusion. If we act in obedience to honour the Lord by responding to His call to corporate prayer in 1 Timothy 2:1, He will honour us by taking control, producing order and granting wisdom to those who lead.

"CLEAN HANDS AND A PURE HEART"

The intercessor must stand before the Lord in a priestly capacity, urging and pleading with God on behalf of others. Just as a high calling gives rise to a high level of accountability before the Lord (Luke 12:48; James 3:1), so it also gives rise to a stricter requirement of holiness before Him and a more rigorous experience of the refiner's fire. If we are to have the high privilege of standing regularly in the audience-chamber of the Sovereign Lord, then we must accept that He will deal with our lives and refine us in a thorough way to remove the dross of sin and of fleshly self-will which would hinder and corrupt the fulfilment of the calling.

The Word of God tells us in Psalm 24:3–4 that if we desire to "stand in his holy place" we need to have "clean hands and a pure heart" and to be those who do "not lift up (our) soul to an idol or swear by what is false." Although God does not exclude us from His presence because of our imperfections and unholiness, we nevertheless find that it is only as He deals with hindrances in our lives that we can be led on into greater depths of revelation and become more effective intercessors.

Unconfessed (and often unrecognised) sin is a hindrance in our walk with God (Isaiah 59:2). There are sometimes occasions when we become aware that there is a barrier in the way of His hearing us, and when this is so we need to ask the Holy Spirit to reveal the cause.

In 2 Samuel 21, we read that a famine afflicted Israel, and when King David asked the Lord the reason, he was shown that it was because the land was under the sin of blood-guiltiness, resulting from Saul's treacherous killing of the Gibeonites in breach of Israel's oath to spare them.

The sin had to be dealt with in the Old Covenant fashion of "a life for a life", and it was only when this had been done that we read, in verse 14, "After that, God answered prayer on behalf of the land." When we find that God is clearly not answering prayer, it is often because He is seeking to draw our attention to an area of sin and the need for repentance. One particular area of great importance is that of right relationships. In 1 Peter 3:7 we read specifically that husbands must treat their wives with consideration and respect, "so that nothing will hinder your prayers."

Since we need to have clean hands and a pure heart, we shall find God dealing not only with manifest sin or wrong relationships in our lives, but also digging deep to expose and refine the motives lurking hidden within our hearts. We shall sometimes be shocked as the Holy Spirit uses the Word of God (Hebrews 4:12–13) to reveal to us the true condition and motivation of our inner beings, but it is a necessary work. If we are to be truly effective, the Lord must deal with our fleshly self-will and corrupt motives which will otherwise inevitably cause us to be vulnerable to manipulation by the forces of evil.

IDOLATRY RENDERS US USELESS

Finally, we must note that Psalm 24 specifically mentions the sin of idolatry, the sin which grieves God more than any other. He cannot tolerate allegiance to any false god in our lives, and He must and will expose it to us and call for repentance. Idolatry ensnares us so subtly and those who bow down to idols come under the influence of demonic powers associated with them, as Paul explains in 1 Corinthians 10:19–20. Psalm 115:8 says, "Those who make [idols] will be like them, and so will all who trust in them."

For many years it has been a source of grief to God that so great a weight of the burden of intercession has been carried by the women. The Lord's handmaidens have shown wonderful courage and faithfulness in bearing this awesome responsibility, but the cry has still been coming forth from the Holy Spirit: "Where are the men who should be on the battlefield? Why are they slumbering while the women are bearing the heat and burden of the battle?"

In recent years, I believe God has answered these questions and that the reason revealed is that the majority of men in the church are prevented from functioning as they should because they are in bondage to the idolatry of mammon. Men are too busy pursuing materialism in its various forms – salary, pension, ambition for status, success and promotion, the desire for a larger house or an additional car – and rationalise it by saying that their hard work is all for the well-being of their family, while the plain hard truth is that they are bowing down to a false god.

Jeremiah 2:13 brings revelation of the nature of idolatry, speaking of "two sins". Idolatry has two distinct aspects – one is the obvious action of turning away from God, but the second and less easily recognised as sin is that of actively seeking to find our security from some source other than God. We are easily deceived into thinking we are not doing the first even though we may be doing the second – but Jesus tells us that they are not separable: "Ye cannot serve God and mammon" (Matthew 6:24 KJV).

We need to examine ourselves and choose which master we are going to serve. If we choose rightly, then we shall be able to take up our responsibilities and play our rightful part in the battles which lie ahead. If not, then God will have no choice but to set us aside as useless in His purposes, for James 4:4 says that "Anyone who chooses to be a friend of the world becomes an enemy of God".

QUESTIONS

1. Can intercession rightly be described as a ministry?
2. Do you think that only a few are called to this sort of commitment, or is it that only a few respond to the call?
3. What strategies of harassment have you encountered? How can you gain the victory against them?

4. On the basis of the scripture in Jeremiah 2:13, what are the identifying signs of idolatry? Do you see them in any situation in which you are involved?

CHAPTER 4

HOW SHOULD WE GO ABOUT IT?

When engaging in a spiritual activity, it is often helpful to have a down-to-earth concept of the role which we are actually playing in the functioning of the kingdom of God. Many years ago when I was first learning about intercession, the Holy Spirit explained it to me in terms which I could grasp quite easily, and although the illustration is undoubtedly imperfect and oversimplified, it is offered here in the hope that some may be helped by it.

Intercessory prayer can be likened in a parable to the working of a car. To achieve the desired effect, the wheels in contact with the road need to be turned, and the engine supplies the power to do so. The car's situation is going to be altered as a result of the power being transmitted to the wheels. In this analogy the engine represents the Holy Spirit's power, and the wheels are the situation which needs to be affected. The intercessor is functioning like the clutch and gearbox, harnessing and directing the power to where it is needed.

In a car, this function is under the direct control of the driver; and so it is with intercession. The driver is the Lord, and just as a clutch and gearbox do not direct themselves, neither does the intercessor direct proceedings in any way. The initiative is always with God.

The principle that the initiative is always with God is foundational to every sphere of activity in His kingdom. There is a thread running through the Gospel of John which lays strong emphasis upon it. In John 5:19–20, Jesus said, "I tell you the truth, the Son can do nothing by himself; he can do only what he sees his Father doing, because whatever the Father does the Son also does. For the Father loves the Son and shows him all he does." Again in verse 30, Jesus reaffirms the principle: "I can do nothing on My own initiative ... I do not seek My own will, but the will of Him who sent Me" (NASB).

Similarly in John 7:6 we find that Jesus never acted at the time of His own choosing; and, in verses 16 to 17, that He did not teach His own ideas, but only what He was receiving from the Father. In chapter 8 verse 28 He said that He spoke only what the Father told Him to say, and again in chapter 12 verses 49 and 50, that the Father not only told Him what to say, but also how to say it.

If the Lord Jesus Christ did nothing on His own initiative, but only what He was told to do and in the way He was told to do it, then neither should we, for we are commanded to "walk as Jesus did" (1 John 2:6). This principle applies as much to intercession as to any other activity in God's kingdom. We may be pleading before the Lord just as Moses did, standing in the gap and representing the people of God; but we must not lose sight of the fact that at all times we are first and foremost servants of the Sovereign Lord, and that the initiative in everything must come from Him.

REVERENCE AND AWE

Our effectiveness in the place of intercession will be greatly affected by our approach towards the Lord with whom we are dealing. Although we are indeed children coming to our Father, we are also exercising the right to enter the audience-chamber of the Creator and Sovereign of the Universe, and it is right to do so with a proper sense of reverence. We have tended in the period of the Charismatic Renewal movement towards emphasizing the Fatherhood of God to the point of overfamiliarity, and in so doing we have lost sight of the fact that it is the fear of the Lord which is the beginning of wisdom (Proverbs 9:10).

Hebrews 12:28–29 says, "let us be thankful, and so worship God acceptably with reverence and awe, for our 'God is a consuming fire.'" In Isaiah 66:2, God says, "This is the one I esteem: he who is humble and contrite in spirit, and trembles at my word." If we wish to prevail with God, we should remember that there is a right way to approach the King of kings, and it is not that of matey familiarity.

We should come into the Lord's presence in a state of worship. In Habakkuk 2:20 we read: "the LORD is in His holy temple; let all the earth hush and keep silence before Him" (Amplified). Silence as an expression of awe and reverence can be the highest form of worship possible. I remember on one occasion hearing a word of rebuke from the Holy Spirit, in which the Lord was asking: "If you had an audience with an earthly monarch, would you not have the courtesy to be silent and wait for him to lead the conversation? Why, then, is it that my people rush into my presence with noise, singing songs about me but ignoring my presence and giving me no opportunity to speak to them of what is on my heart concerning them?"

When we come to the place of intercession, it is good to

worship the Lord in silence. "Be still, and know that I am God" (Psalm 46:10), for it is only in the stillness that we become really aware of His presence. So many Christians say that they find it hard to listen to God – but how can you listen to Him if you never give Him opportunity to speak, or you are so busy listening to the clamour of the world that you are deafened to the "still small voice" in your inner being which is His characteristic way of communicating directly with us? If we are not hearing from God's throne, then how are we to intercede effectively? It is virtually impossible. We must learn the discipline of being still before Him.

GOD KNOWS HIS OWN AGENDA

When coming to a regular time set aside for intercession, it is good to be as unhurried as possible. God is not a clock-watcher and it is a delight to Him when His people give Him time. It is very difficult to intercede effectively unless first we take the time to become quiet before the Lord and to receive an awareness of His presence and to allow the Spirit to calm our busy hearts and minds with His peace. This is a time when it proves of immense value first to pray silently in a tongue and then to listen for His voice; the mind is inactive and at rest, while the spirit is being edified and, as it were, "fine-tuned" to be ready to start hearing from God and responding to what He is saying. It is better to spend forty-five minutes, if necessary, becoming quiet before the Lord, and only fifteen minutes of actual prayer, than to spend an entire hour off-balance and confused, not knowing whether you are praying effectively or totally missing the target.

We need to come into the place of intercession with no preconceived agenda (unless of course the Lord has already made the matter for prayer abundantly clear). Otherwise, when we keep a regular appointment with the Lord, we must allow Him to choose the agenda. We may have on our own heart a burden of love and deep concern for some particular person or situation; but we may well find, as we begin to wait upon the Lord, that He reassures us that He already has that matter in hand and that He wants to communicate to us a quite different burden from His heart.

It is for God to

1. Give us the burden.
2. Give any necessary revelation about the circumstances.
3. Reveal His will for dealing with it.
4. Inspire the prayers He wants to answer which will result in the accomplishing of His will.
5. Inspire any practical action we need to take, or any strategy of spiritual warfare – e.g. fasting. The initiative in this also must be His, and not our own good idea.

SHARING IN THE GRIEF OF GOD

As experience grows, the intercessor begins to have an increasing awareness of what is coming from the heart of God. Normally there will be a sense of peace; but often there is also much grief. Jesus wept over Jerusalem (Luke 19:41–44), and today God's heart is grieving over the state of His church and His world. The intercessor is frequently called to share in God's grief, at least in the measure that we can bear.

Many Christians enjoy songs taken from Isaiah 61:3 about receiving from the Lord beauty instead of ashes, the oil of joy instead of mourning, and the garment of praise in place of the spirit of heaviness – but often we do not seem to have become aware of the context, which is that God gives these things to those who "grieve in Zion". It is they who will also have the privilege of rebuilding ancient ruins, restoring devastated places and renewing the ruined cities (v. 4).

THE EXAMPLE OF NEHEMIAH

Nehemiah was such a man and the first chapter of the book of Nehemiah continues one of the great classic prayers of intercession recorded in Scripture. It repays much study:

1. He wanted to know about the state of God's chosen people and city – he cared, so God provided the knowledge about the situation (Nehemiah 1:1–3).

2. He was prepared to humble himself before God and to spend a lengthy time sharing the Lord's grief and concern (Nehemiah 1:4).

3. He prayed, pleading with God for His people (Nehemiah 1:5–6, 11).

4. He identified with the sins of the nation of which he was a part, confessing how they had offended against the Lord and disobeyed His Word (Nehemiah 1:6–7).

5. He based his pleading on the Word of God, reminding Him of His revealed will in the situation and urging Him to act accordingly (Nehemiah 1:8–10).

6. Finally, in chapter 2, he received the opportunity to be a part of the answer to his own prayer. He had grieved over the situation and stood in the gap for the nation, and God chose to send him back to be a rebuilder of the ruins, according exactly with the principle which we have just examined in Isaiah 61:3–4.

Every one of these points is significant for our instruction in the ways of intercession. In particular we should note the principle in verse 6 of the intercessor identifying with the sinful situation of which he was a part, even though there is no indication that he personally had committed any such sins – a principle which is underlined even more fully in Daniel 9:4–19, another great intercessory prayer which is worth much careful examination.

Each of us is a part of certain corporate bodies; we are members of the nation, of the church as a whole, of our local fellowship, of our family; and when we are called to pray for something of which we are a part, it is right for us to identify fully with every aspect of the situation, including confession of sin. God is often waiting and longing for somebody to confess the sin so that He may extend the grace of forgiveness, and at those times it is a significant part of the intercessory task to do so.

BEARING THE BURDEN

We need also to be aware that in addition to the specific prayers which an intercessor may pray concerning a troubled situation, there can be times when their spoken intercession ceases but the Holy Spirit causes them to stand in the gap by means of bearing in their own direct personal experience a measure of the suffering involved in that situation. This is often the case when one is called to a deep commitment to stand alongside a suffering person or group of people.

This is not the same as sharing the burden of God's own grief, about which we have already spoken; but rather it is a direct identification with the trials of those who are suffering, often in the form of sharing in a measure in the same spiritual or emotional distress with which they are afflicted. To take one specific example – this is a common experience for those who pray for Israel, God's persecuted and suffering people of the Old Covenant. God identifies with His people in their afflictions (Isaiah 63:9) and the intercessor is often called similarly to share to some degree in bearing the burden of suffering.

This is also what the Holy Spirit is doing when He "intercedes for us with groans that words cannot express" (Romans 8:26); every aspect of intercession is an expression of an activity in which God Himself takes a full part. We are never alone in our intercession.

WITH THE SPIRIT AND THE WORD

Finally in this chapter, we must consider how and in what words we should actually pray the prayer of intercession. One cannot of course lay down hard and fast rules, but two points are particularly worth noting:

1. The spiritual gift of tongues is often indispensable and should be used frequently. In times of weariness or perplexity, a period of praying with the Spirit will refresh and build us up inwardly, after which it proves much easier for one's mind to be enlightened. It is also an invaluable practice at times when one is aware that there is a real spiritual battle involved in the situation – the Holy Spirit knows what to pray much better than we do!

2. Praying the actual words of Scripture is a powerful and effective way of interceding. The Word of God is indeed "alive and powerful ... sharper than ... [a] two-edged sword" (Hebrews 4:12 NLT). The Holy Spirit will often lead to an appropriate scripture for the situation. This should hardly surprise us because in Psalm 138:2 we read that God has "exalted above all things [His] name and [His] word".

It may be helpful to conclude with a specific example. Some years ago, there was an occasion when the ministry team with whom I worked was involved in a weekend mission. We arrived on the Thursday evening to learn that the police were expecting serious rioting in the town on the Saturday. They had received a warning that a local demonstration march would be swelled by large numbers of reinforcements being brought in by the busload from other places specifically to stir up violence; 20,000 people were expected to be involved.

A day of prayer and fasting was called on the Friday, and during the day the Holy Spirit brought to us a word of Scripture (Psalm 55:9–11) through a lady who lived locally. Accordingly, we interceded on the basis of asking the Lord to confuse the evil plans which had been made. We retired to bed on the Friday night, not knowing what God would do, but confident that He had heard us. It was towards the middle of March.

On the Saturday morning, to our amazement, we awoke to see a substantial layer of snow on the ground. It continued to snow all day and was so deep that the coachloads of reinforcements were never able to arrive. The demonstration consisted of only 2,000 people in total and passed off entirely peacefully. It was only later that we discovered that the snowstorm only covered an area of about thirty miles around the town. God had indeed heard our prayers.

God knew the situation and knew exactly how to deal with it. He always does! The task of the intercessor is simply to pray the prayer which He is wanting to answer.

QUESTIONS

1. How would it affect the functioning of your fellowship or prayer group if you no longer did anything on your own initiative?
2. Would it enhance the quality of your worship to begin by being silent in the presence of the Lord?
3. Is the Lord wanting you to identify with any sin in a corporate group to which you belong, asking His forgiveness as a representative of the whole?

4. Do you need to seek God's strategy to know how to pray concerning some seemingly impossible situation confronting you or your fellowship?

CHAPTER 5

BY REVELATION

It is basic to the functioning of the kingdom of God that all activity which is truly of that kingdom is conceived in the heart of God, initiated by the Word of God and carried out by the power and under the direction of the Holy Spirit. Any activity, including intercession, which is simply the fruit of human good ideas, initiated by us or carried out in our own ways and strength, is a work of the flesh and not of the Holy Spirit; it is a manifestation of us "doing our own thing" which is, in fact, the basis of all sin – Isaiah 53:6 says that "each of us has turned to his own way". Any such activity is of little use in accomplishing the will of God; indeed, it can often be a positive hindrance to the Lord in the working out of His purposes.

Our God has certain ways in which He delights to work. He runs His kingdom by first revealing His purposes and then carrying them out, a principle underlined in Genesis 18:17, Isaiah 48:3–5 and Amos 3:7–8.

The kingdom of God is a kingdom in which we must walk

in the light of the revelation which God gives to us. When we understand these things, they will revolutionise our praying.

The very foundation of all intercessory prayer must be the heart-attitude which says continually to the Lord: "Thy will be done." True intercessors never stand knowingly against the will of God, but seek revelation of what God thinks concerning the matter in hand and desires to do about it, so that they can pray in harmony with God's own purposes. They seek to pray in accordance with the revealed will of God, so as to move His hand in power to do that which He already purposes.

We need to walk as Jesus walked (1 John 2:6). The motivation for the whole life and ministry of the Lord Jesus Christ can be summarised in three verses from John's Gospel – 6:38: "I have come down from heaven not to do my will but to do the will of him who sent me"; 12:27: "Now my heart is troubled, and what shall I say? 'Father, save me from this hour'? No, it was for this very reason I came to this hour. Father, glorify your name!"; and 17:4: "I have brought you glory on earth by completing the work you gave me to do." Jesus' purpose was that of total obedience to do the will of the Father and to glorify His name; everything else was secondary.

Understood in the light of the motivation of Jesus, we begin to understand our function as intercessors in a new way. There is a higher purpose in intercessory prayer than that of changing wrong situations, or easing suffering and oppression. Good and necessary as those objectives are, they are matters which God deals with in His own way and at His own time. He who knows all things knows how to do what is right (Genesis 18:25), and does not need us to tell Him what we think He should do, or how He should do it (Isaiah 40:13–14; Isaiah 45:11)!

Although we are called to stand in the gap on behalf of others, in love and compassionate concern, identifying with the situation and even suffering alongside it, yet even so our principal motive must be to get the will of God done, whatever that may prove to be. We need the Holy Spirit to reveal the will of God and how He wants to carry it out, so that we can then cooperate by praying and urging Him to accomplish the revealed purposes of His own heart.

GOD DESIRES US TO KNOW HIS WILL

We are mistaken if we think that God answers our prayers simply because we have felt the burden to pray. 1 John 5:14–15 tells us that "if we ask anything according to his will, he hears us. And if we know that he hears us ... we know that we have what we asked of him". To pray in the name of Jesus is to pray according to the Father's will, because then and only then we will be praying in agreement with Jesus. The prayers which God answers are those which He first inspires within us; the initiative must always be from Him.

So we come to the very heart of the matter – how should we pray? In every new situation we need to be like the first disciples, saying, "Lord, teach us how to pray." When we come to Him in humility, acknowledging the truth that without Him we can do nothing, not even pray effectively, we shall find the Holy Spirit coming to our aid without fail.

How can we receive revelation and know the will of God? We need to know "the mind of Christ" (1 Corinthians 2:16) – but how?

It is not really difficult, as some seem to think. We do not need to strive. God wants His people to know His will. He loves to communicate with us. Certainly there are such things as deceiving spirits, and also the vain imaginings of our own mind; but although we must be alert to test what we are hearing in our spirits, we need to have our emphasis upon a Father who is utterly faithful. We should trust the faithfulness of Him who will not give us a stone when we ask for bread, or a snake when we ask for fish (Matthew 7:9–10); and who promises that if we ask Him for wisdom, He will gladly give it to us (James 1:5). We should not be overwhelmed by fear of being deceived, or unbelieving about God giving us wisdom.

He is our perfect Father and He is totally in charge, seated on His throne, so we should trust Him expectantly.

WE MUST LISTEN

We need to learn how to be a listening people – those who are disciplined to be still and quiet before Him and to give Him time. We Christians in our Western culture are so often impatient and hasty, but God wants to teach us differently. There is nothing more Scriptural than waiting – waiting upon God and waiting for God. Isaiah 64:4 says that He "works for those who wait for him" (RSV). Jeremiah, needing what seemed an urgent answer, had to wait ten days (Jeremiah 42:7).

Jesus said, "My sheep listen to my voice; I know them, and they follow me" (John 10:27), but in practice how are we to recognise His voice? There are certain hallmarks of the genuine voice of God, and they are learned only by experience. God rarely shouts; His Spirit speaks in a "gentle whisper" such as Elijah heard (1 Kings 19:12). It is very rarely an audible voice, for God loves to speak to us "heart to heart"; His Spirit communicates directly into our own spirit, and the impression of what He is saying then comes into our mind. There is often a strong sense of His presence, which again we discern in our spirit; but when it is truly God, although there may be a sense of great awe, there is never a sense of fear on the ordinary human level.

God speaks "peace unto his people" (Psalm 85:8 KJV). His voice, although quiet, calm and peaceful, is nevertheless also characterised by a sense of great authority.

Yet God is not limited to speaking directly into our spirit. He also speaks in a variety of other ways. He may give a word of prophecy, or a picture or vision which requires interpretation. (We should never put our own immediate human interpretation on a picture, however obvious it may appear to be – always ask the Lord to give right understanding.)

God will also often speak by drawing attention to a word of Scripture. In all these situations it is the case that "Two are better than one" (Ecclesiastes 4:9), for we can pray and confirm (or deny) to each other that we are receiving the same witness from the Holy Spirit. God wants us to have assured faith, confident in what we believe we are receiving from Him, so that we shall be able to pray with a sense of certainty that we are acting in agreement with what He wants.

CAN WE TRUST WHAT WE HEAR?

Most important of all, perhaps, in identifying the voice of the Lord, is being able to recognise how He speaks – the sort of things He would be likely to say. We need not only to recognise God's voice, however it may come to us, but also to identify the content as being genuine. This is the area of greatest difficulty for many of us, and often we can miss what God is trying to say to us because we fail to identify the content as being from Him. Why should this be?

The problem is that of lack of familiarity with the ways of God, and overfamiliarity with the ways of the world. In Isaiah 55:8–9, the Scripture tells us plainly that God's thoughts and His ways are not the same as ours; they operate on a higher plane altogether. In order to be able to identify God's thoughts and ways, it is essential that we should take to heart the Scripture in Romans 12:2: "Do not conform any longer to the pattern of this world, but be transformed by the renewing of your mind. Then you will be able to test and approve what God's will is – his good, pleasing and perfect will."

This is vital for any Christian in these days when we are surrounded on all sides by the shoutings of the world system. If that is all we usually hear, we shall not easily recognise God's voice when He speaks. We may even cast it aside as ridiculous – "the foolishness of God is wiser than man's wisdom, and the weakness of God is stronger than man's strength" (1 Corinthians 1:25) – but unless we are familiar with the "foolish" ways of God, how are we to recognise that His wisdom is actually in what He is trying to say to us? If Joshua had applied human reasoning to God's strategy for taking Jericho when it was given to him (Joshua 6:2–5), he would have discarded it as absurd and the city would not have been taken.

God's ways and strategies often do appear extraordinary to us, and unless our minds have been renewed so as to be in the habit of thinking in the ways of God, then we may find ourselves ignorantly rejecting what He is revealing to us or telling us to do.

How can our minds be renewed? There is only one way, and we neglect it at our peril. It is through the Word of God being ministered to our spirits by the illuminating power of the Holy Spirit. There is no other way, and there is no short cut. It is vital, if we are to be effective intercessors, that our minds are steeped in the Word of God, because only then will we be able to understand His thoughts and His ways. Do not let anything crowd out of your life your regular intake of the Word of God and your times of communing with the Holy Spirit. If necessary, throw away all the other books and tapes, not to mention the television. You need the thoughts of God feeding your heart as vitally as you need your daily food to sustain the life of your body – but you can manage perfectly well without most human opinion and the deafening shouts of the world.

PRAYING IN OBEDIENCE TO GOD'S REVELATION

When we have reached the point of confidence as to what the Holy Spirit wants us to pray, we must then in obedience pray in the way which He has shown. Often it is easy and a delight to do – but sometimes it is not so. We referred in a previous chapter to the prayers of Elijah: "The prayer of a righteous man is powerful and effective" (James 5:16).

But consider what he was asked to pray. Burdened by the sins of idolatry which Ahab and Jezebel were introducing throughout Israel (1 Kings 16:30–33), Elijah must have been crying out to God to deal with this situation and turn the hearts of the people back to Him. This was entirely what the Lord wanted, but how Elijah must have shuddered when he became aware that the means of doing so was to be a drought upon the land (James 5:17). He was being asked to pray for a catastrophe upon his own people, and one in which he would also have to share the suffering. It is a measure of Elijah's stature as a faithful man of God that he did not flinch from the responsibility, but it should make the point for us that it can be hard for an intercessor to pray according to the will of God, even with the assurance of long-term good results. It is not unusual to be faced with a situation which is a mess and to long to pray for immediate improvement, only to find the Holy Spirit telling us that in God's wisdom it must become worse before it can begin to improve. At such times we can only grit our teeth and submit to pray in co-operation with the will and wisdom of God, even when we simply do not understand the reasons.

It is important to walk very closely with God, seeking always to sense what is on His heart. There are often times when God states His intention about a situation where sin is calling for righteous judgment, but nevertheless He strongly desires that the intercessor should plead with Him to relent. We saw examples of this in a previous chapter – Abraham pleading for Sodom (Genesis 18), and Moses for the people of Israel (Exodus 32).

At the same time, however, we must understand clearly that there can also be times when the Lord will make plain to the one who is interceding that His mind is made up, and that His will in the matter is now unalterable. Thus in Amos 7:1–9, Amos was twice able to intercede successfully to avert God's stated intention of judgment, but on the third occasion he was not given the opportunity to do so. Three times in the book of Jeremiah (7:16; 11:14; 14:11–12) we find that the prophet had the terrible experience of being forbidden even to pray for the people; because of the sins of King Manasseh (2 Kings 21:1–16; see Jeremiah 15:1–4), the Lord's patience had at last run out, and in 2 Kings 24:4 we find the awful words: "… and the LORD was not willing to forgive."

There does come a time when an individual, or a church, or a nation has presumed too long upon the Lord's grace and patience, and judgment becomes inevitable. The intercessor must sometimes face that possibility, and if it proves so, he can only bow to the will of God and become silent on the matter. We are only to intercede with God, never against His declared purpose when He has stated His decision to be final.

The most we may then be permitted to do is to plead that in the midst of judgment, God will also remember mercy.

Questions

1. Do you think it would make a difference to how you pray if you were first to seek to know the will of God for every situation?

2. 1 Corinthians 2:16 says, "we have the mind of Christ". Do you know what He thinks in every situation which confronts you? If not, what are the hindrances?

3. If you thought you heard God telling you to do something which seems ridiculous, would you dismiss it as nonsense? If not, how would you respond? How would you ensure that it was really from God?

4. Would you be willing, like Elijah, to pray for an apparent disaster if God asked you to do so?

CHAPTER 6

IT IS WARFARE

In 2 Kings 6:15–17, we read how God met with the need of Elisha's servant in a miraculous way. Elisha and his servant were in the city of Dothan, surrounded by the army of the King of Syria who wanted to capture Elisha. The servant was fearful at the sight of this army of horses and chariots, but Elisha reassured him, "Those who are with us are more than those who are with them." Perhaps this reassurance was not sufficient, however; for Elisha then prayed and the Lord enabled the servant to see that there was a heavenly army of horses and chariots of fire surrounding them with protection.

If our eyes were to be similarly opened, we would be both encouraged and appalled at what we would see. We are caught up in the midst of a battle of staggering proportions and ferocity being waged unseen all around us. This battle is also manifested powerfully in many ways in our daily experience, but we do not always recognise what is going on.

Ephesians 6:12 enlightens us. Often we think we are in a battle against human beings, or being affected by natural disasters, but behind human strife and conflict and other catastrophes lies the true cause, the spiritual battle between two opposing kingdoms: "For our struggle is not against flesh and blood, but against the rulers, against the authorities, against the powers of this dark world and against the spiritual forces of evil in the heavenly realms."

WHO CONTROLS HUMAN THOUGHTS?

2 Corinthians 10:3-4 says, "though we live in the world, we do not wage war as the world does. The weapons we fight with are not the weapons of the world. On the contrary, they have divine power to demolish strongholds." Intercessory prayer is one of the spiritual weapons which we must employ in the spiritual war in which we are involved. It is the prayer which moves the hand of God in divine power against the strongholds which are built by Satan's kingdom of darkness in human hearts and in human society. This Satan does principally by exercising control over the minds of people. He who can control the mind can control the whole person. That is why the following verse in 2 Corinthians 10 goes on to say, "We demolish arguments and every pretension that sets itself up against the knowledge of God, and we take captive every thought to make it obedient to Christ" (v. 5).

The battle is to establish the truth of God against the lies of Satan. In these days of greatly increasing deception, there has come an astonishing release of occult powers seeking to control people's minds by subtle and deceptive means – this is the principal aim of the New Age movement. "… as [a man] thinketh in his heart, so is he" says the Word of God (Proverbs 23:7 KJV), and captive hearts and minds can be released only by the power of God, demolishing the holds upon them in answer to prayer. If we do not know how to use our spiritual weapons, we are helpless in the face of the onslaught of evil in these days.

TWO KINGDOMS IN OPPOSITION

It is warfare, and it is not going to stop until the Lord Jesus returns. We have already seen that the chief aim of the intercessor is to be an effective instrument in getting the will of God accomplished in the situation about which we are asked to pray – and getting the will of God done is not an easy matter, because Satan's kingdom opposes it at every point.

The kingdom of God is "not of this world" (John 18:36). The world system can be defined as human society organizing itself without reference to God, and therefore in rebellion against the Creator and Sovereign Lord. This is the dark kingdom which Satan is able to rule through his demonic forces, controlling those who are deceived into thinking they are free to direct their own destiny; Jesus revealed Satan as being the unseen controlling "prince of this world" (John 12:31; 16:11).

Yet those two Scriptures also refer specifically to Satan's defeat and condemnation, which was sealed at Calvary. As Christians, we know we are on the side of victory. Why, then, this prolonged and bitter warfare? Why the need for struggle and travail in the place of intercession, agonising to see God's will done, to see captive people and situations released? Why does God not just push Satan aside? After all, He is the Sovereign Lord. Why does He not simply forbid any opposition, or even arise from His seat, speak His word, and consign all His enemies to final destruction?

That day will come; and sometimes God does forbid opposition, as for example we read in Exodus chapters 7 and 8. When God brought judgment on Egypt by plagues of various sorts, He allowed Pharaoh's magicians at first to produce identical results by their occult powers (Exodus 7:11-12, 22; 8:7). However, when it came to the plague of gnats, God intervened. The magicians found they could no longer produce the results (8:18), and testified to Pharaoh that they now knew that it was God Himself who was bringing the plagues upon Egypt (v. 19).

GOD IS TRAINING OVERCOMERS

God does not often intervene like that, however – and we have to learn that it is actually in His purposes and for our benefit that the battle has to be fought, long and exhausting though it often proves. God wants His people to have to face opposition. It causes us to grow and become strong and mature in spirit. It tests our faith and obedience. In each of the letters to the seven churches in Revelation 2 and 3, the commendation and the promises are to those who "overcome" and do His will to the end (e.g. Revelation 2:26). God wants us to be "overcomers". He continues to permit Satan's activity so that we can learn total dependence on Jesus and come into the spiritually mature state of knowing and acknowledging that in Him alone can we prevail.

God is producing warriors – men and women (and children also) of courage and determination: mature, seasoned soldiers. Satan is allowed to oppose and operate in subtle ways so that we become strong and mature in exercising discernment (Hebrews 5:14); he is allowed to harass and hinder us, as he did with Job, because it fulfils God's purpose of testing and refining us to see if we will continue to trust, obey and walk with Him even in difficult, wilderness situations, and sometimes in utter perplexity (see e.g. Deuteronomy 8:2; Isaiah 50:10). King David was prepared for his task by being sorely tested by Satan's forces operating against him through the malevolent heart of Saul, a story running through the entire second half of the book of 1 Samuel.

THE ROLE OF THE INTERCESSOR

In the spiritual battle being fought today, the work of the intercessors is vital. Their prayers operate to build a wall of God's protection around others who are fighting in exposed and vulnerable positions. They serve as an artillery bombardment to weaken the opposition which the front line infantry must attack, and they act like air cover to protect them while they are doing so. Without the company of intercessors, this spiritual army has little hope of success, or sometimes even of survival; but with the powers of God released against the enemy in response to persevering intercession, protection is provided and victory comes.

In this battle, those fighting on the field prevail when prayer is prevailing with God. When Joshua fought the Amalekites (Exodus 17:8–13), the Israelites were winning all the time that Moses' hands were held up in prayer, but began to lose if he lowered them. Finally he was so tired that Aaron and Hur had to support his hands until the victory was complete. Intercessors need to cooperate and support one another, for the work involved is no light task, but often an exhausting labour of dogged perseverance.

FASTING

The place of fasting in intercession is of importance. When references to fasting occur in Scripture, it is always in the context of either grieving before the Lord, or of humbling before Him, and often both together.

Both aspects are thoroughly appropriate in the work of intercession. We have referred earlier to the fact that the intercessor (such as Nehemiah) is often called to share in God's grief; and at the very outset of this book we made reference to the familiar Scripture in 2 Chronicles 7:14: "if my people, who are called by my name, will humble themselves and pray ... then will I hear from heaven ..."

Fasting is effective in communicating to the Lord both grief and humility, and as an indication that we mean serious business with Him. There must be a note of caution, however. We have seen that Jesus did nothing on His own initiative, and therefore neither must we. As with other matters, fasting must be an activity initiated by the directing of the Holy Spirit. It is of little value if it is done as our own good idea, or as a self-imposed regulation. These are just works of the flesh, as with the Pharisee who fasted "twice a week" but cut no ice at all with God because of his self-righteousness (Luke 18:12).

Even worse is fasting which is undertaken as a religious exercise with the idea that God will be impressed and therefore respond in the way we desire. Our Father has no time for empty religious activity and sees straight through it as being a sham and a façade. We learn what He feels about it when we read in Isaiah 58 that fasting, without justice and righteousness to one's neighbour, serves only to bring God's stern rebuke.

THE PLACE OF PRAISE

There has been some confusion and disagreement in recent years concerning the place which praise should occupy in intercession and spiritual warfare. Some have seemed to be under the impression that praise is a complete formula for victory in itself, but the weight of Scripture does not support this view.

Praise is never a substitute for prayer, important though it is. We have already referred to the 1906 prophecy warning that there would come a time when people would praise the God to whom they no longer pray. I have to confess to being uneasy about the use of the term "praise warfare", which makes it sound as if praise is like a chemical bomb which gasses the opposition and brings total victory at once! There is a danger that we can easily, without realising what we are actually doing, fall into the trap of using praise as an instrument to try to manipulate God into taking action. To do this is to act out of an utterly false motivation which is neither pleasing to the Lord nor a credit to ourselves.

Much has been made of the account of King Jehoshaphat's victory in 2 Chronicles 20, where in verse 22 we read that "As they began to sing and praise, the LORD set ambushes against the men … who were invading Judah, and they were defeated." But if the whole chapter is read, we see Jehoshaphat and all Judah coming together, fasting in humility before the Lord (vv. 3–4, 13); we find Jehoshaphat uttering an inspired prayer of intercession (vv. 6–12) and confessing utter helplessness; and then we find the Lord responding through a prophet to encourage and instruct the whole assembly (vv. 14–17).

Reading what Jahaziel prophesied, we see in verse 17 that God had already given the victory, and that the only condition was the obedience of going out to face the enemy, taking up their positions, and waiting to see the Lord act in deliverance.

No wonder they praised! Who would not at such a wonderful response from the Lord, and promise of deliverance? But we cannot be faithful to Scripture and say that praise won the victory. Praise was the appropriate response in that case to the victory which was already certain, provided they obeyed what they had been told to do.

However, there is a place for praise as an effective instrument of battle in a particular type of situation. In Psalm 8:2 we read, "From the lips of children and infants you have ordained praise because of your enemies, to silence the foe and the avenger." Praise to God is mightily effective in silencing the enemy's shoutings, and experience suggests that it is particularly so when those shoutings are in the form of lies and accusations.

If we are sensitive and open to the leading and direction of the Holy Spirit, He will direct us rightly and show us the times and situations when it is appropriate to employ praise in the battle. He often does so, for example, in the context of the Lord authorising a corporate onslaught in prayer against major powers and principalities – but a word of caution. Do not launch attacks against the enemy forces on your own initiative – you may not like the retaliation! God is the Commander of His own army, and He alone must plan the strategy and give the orders. Like Jesus, we must do only what we are aware that the Father is doing.

THE CALL TO PERSEVERE

Finally, we are called in intercession to persevere, and in Daniel 10 we are shown one reason why it is so often necessary. Daniel had been given a great revelation in a vision, but he needed understanding of its meaning. It was very important that he should receive this understanding, for it concerned the end times and was to be incorporated into Scripture (in chapters 11 and 12) for the benefit of future generations. Consequently there was much opposition to him receiving the understanding.

We find in verse 2 that Daniel prayed and fasted for three weeks, until an angelic messenger finally came to him. The messenger explained (v. 12) that although God had heard and answered his prayer for understanding on the very day that he began to pray and humble himself before Him, yet the messenger had been delayed, held up in a battle with the great ruling satanic power over Persia, until he was relieved by the angel Michael and released to go on his way.

This delay had been for twenty-one days, the exact length of time during which Daniel had been persevering in fasting and prayer, beseeching God to give the understanding he needed to have. The angelic messenger also told him that he would be returning to fight against the satanic prince over Persia, that the ruling prince over Greece was also involved, and that he and Michael stood alone against them in the unseen battle in the heavenly places.

Daniel had to persevere. When we believe we are interceding according to the will of God and yet there are sometimes long, inexplicable delays, we also need to persevere, refusing to give up until we are aware that the will of God has been accomplished. It is warfare, and the joy of victory is for those who pray and wait and agonise, persevere and overcome, knowing that God is with them from beginning to end.

QUESTIONS

1. When in conflict with other people, should you ask the Lord to reveal what unseen powers are at work in the situation?

2. What weapons do you use in spiritual battles? Does the Holy Spirit direct how and when you are to use them?

3. When Christian leaders are disgraced through moral corruption, do you think it is the result of a deliberate line of satanic attack upon them? Might they have been able to avoid the trap if they had had greater protection in prayer?

4. Those who are in the "front line" of the battle are vulnerable to many kinds of attack. Is the Lord asking you to be specially committed to support and protect in prayer any particular person or group of people?

Chapter 7

The Intercession of the Great High Priest

We have seen in an earlier chapter that the ministry of intercession is both a priestly role and a divine activity. As in every other aspect of our walk before God, the Lord Jesus is Himself our role model and supreme example of what it means to be a true intercessor. We are His co-workers, and just as He could do only what He saw the Father doing (John 5:19), so we also will only be effective to the extent that we are walking in harmony with Him; for as He said, "apart from me you can do nothing" (John 15:5).

IDENTIFICATION
At the very heart of effective intercession lies the principle of identification: understanding the purposes of God's heart by the revelation which comes from the Holy Spirit; and being willing to be entirely associated – in heart-understanding and often in direct experience – with the circumstances which call forth the need to stand in the gap before the throne of grace.

Aaron, as the Israelite high priest, demonstrates symbolically the importance of identification with those for whom he was responsible before the Lord. He did so every time he put on his ceremonial garments. On the shoulders of the ephod he bore two memorial stones of onyx, each having engraved on them the names of six of the tribes of Israel, while on the breastplate were mounted twelve precious stones, each also engraved with the name of one of the twelve tribes (Exodus 28:9–21) so that "Whenever Aaron enters the Holy Place, he will bear the names of the sons of Israel over his heart on the breastpiece of decision as a continuing memorial before the LORD" (Exodus 28:29).

Aaron, and all subsequent holders of the office of high priest, had to be totally identified with those for whom they made representation before the Lord. The most dramatic example of doing so came annually on Yom Kippur, the Day of Atonement, when the high priest had the awe-inspiring responsibility of going alone behind the curtain into the presence of God in the Holy of Holies, taking incense and sprinkling the blood of a bull and of a goat on the atonement cover to make atonement for the sins of the nation, which were then temporarily covered by the shed blood (Leviticus 16:1–17).

The awesome solemnity of this duty of the high priest to come before the Lord with blood on behalf of his fellow Israelites is underlined by the fact that even he – and he alone – was permitted to enter the Holy of Holies only on that one occasion during the year. Nobody else was allowed at any time to go behind the separating curtain, and the seriousness of this intercessory action, identifying with the sin of the whole nation, is further emphasised by the somewhat macabre practice of tying a rope to the leg of the high priest in order to be able to pull out his body lest he should die in the Most Holy Place before the Lord – for in that event, it would have been irretrievable, no other man being permitted to enter there at any time or for any reason.

By this annual action on Yom Kippur, the high priest "was numbered with...and made intercession for the transgressors" (Isaiah 53:12) – an act of identification which was to find its complete prophetic fulfilment at Calvary, when the separating curtain in the Temple was ripped in two and Jesus made a permanent atonement with His own shed blood for the sins of the world which He was bearing in His own person on the cross. His act of identification with all sinners qualified Him to become the unique permanent intercessor standing at the right hand of the Father to plead effectively for us on the ground of the shed blood of His cross.

THE COST OF IDENTIFICATION

True intercessors are called to pay a high personal price in the process of fulfilling the calling of God. The depth of identification needed may call for great personal sacrifice. They must often be willing to share in a great burden of pain, grief and concern over people and situations, even to the point of experiencing in their own person a level of agony which can often be hard to bear. They must be willing to sacrifice their own interests to whatever extent may be necessary, even to including their own lives. We know, of course, that this was the price paid by Jesus in fulfilment of the messianic prophecy of Isaiah 53, and that same willingness is found in the intercession of Moses (Exodus 32:30–34), and in the agonised cry of Paul on behalf of his people (Romans 9:3).

Yet for Jesus, this ultimate sacrifice was not the whole, but only the culmination, of His sacrificial intercession for us. The whole of His life on earth involved a permanent costly identification, as we shall examine subsequently.

THE EXAMPLE OF ESTHER

Esther (or Hadassah, to give her her Hebrew name) is a permanent illustration for us of what it means to be called to exercise an effective intercessory role by living it out in a costly way of life and action.

Taking place some thirty years before Nehemiah's return from the Babylonian exile to rebuild the walls of Jerusalem, the central theme of the book of Esther is the saving of the Jews in Persia through the courage of a young Jewish woman. She had been placed in a key position in the court of the Persian King Ahasuerus and proved herself willing to risk her life as an instrument in God's hand to intercede with the king for her fellow Jews.

All the Jews living in Persia at that time came under threat of genocide because of the murderous anti-Semitism of Haman, an Amalekite descended from King Agag, whose life Saul in disobedience had spared (1 Samuel 15:1–33). Haman's particular hatred of Mordecai, Esther's cousin and guardian, gave rise to a plot to kill not only him but all the Jews in the Persian Empire.

Esther was, by God's provision, the only Jew in a position to be able to obtain access to the king to expose Haman's evil intention. To do so, however, would involve risking her life if Ahasuerus did not show her favour. Nevertheless, although afraid, she was convinced by Mordecai that she was called to stand in the gap before the king, and intercede for her people.

What was asked of her was daunting, but she displayed the heart of a true intercessor. Despite the risk even of losing her life, she was willing to identify with her people, revealing herself to the king as a Jew (Esther 7:3–4; 8:3–6), and being willing to pay the supreme price for her action if that should be asked of her: "I will go to the king, even though it is against the law. And if I perish, I perish" (Esther 4:16).

Esther's willingness to identify entirely with her threatened people and to intercede at whatever the cost resulted in the hand of God being moved to give her favour with Ahasuerus; to save and honour both Esther and her fellow Jews; and to destroy their deadly enemy, Haman, on his own gallows which he had constructed in order to hang Mordecai. Her action is commemorated annually in the Feast of Purim.

THE INTERCESSORY LIFE OF JESUS

We have said already that the ministry of true intercession is a divine activity and an act of selfless sacrificial love. Its roots and motivation are to be found entirely in the unfathomable depths of compassion in the heart of God; and as in all other activity of eternal significance and value, our role model is the Lord Jesus Himself, the complete revelation of the person and nature of the Father.

He is the one who "always lives to make intercession for them" (Hebrews 7:25 NKJV), standing in the gap as mediator before the Father on behalf of fallen humanity, pleading the case for us to be forgiven and declared righteous on the basis of the shedding of His blood when He sacrificed Himself at the cross of Calvary: "… he poured out his life unto death, and was numbered with the transgressors. For he bore the sin of many, and made intercession for the transgressors" (Isaiah 53:12).

These awe-inspiring words express the central core of the divine activity which has delivered us from the penalty of eternal death, achieved forgiveness and reconciliation with the Father, and brought us through the torn veil into the very presence of God with an assurance of everlasting life in His eternal kingdom.

Yet although this was the climax of the intercessory activity of Jesus on our behalf, we are mistaken if we think that Calvary alone constituted the whole of His intercession for us transgressors. Calvary was and is an eternal and complete work in itself; the sacrifice of Jesus as the perfect lamb who took our sins upon Himself and made atonement by the shedding of His own blood stands for ever as the qualification for our forgiveness and salvation. Yet the Great High Priest as our eternal intercessor poured out His life unto death in His identification with us and our human condition from the moment that He left His Father's side and took on human flesh, when conception took place in the womb of a young woman.

It is amazing to realise afresh that the cost to God of achieving our redemption was decided from all eternity and that Jesus, the Word of God, would always have been aware of all that would be asked of Him in the fullness of time. Yet the Scriptures make this plain: He is "the Lamb that was slain from the creation of the world" (Revelation 13:8); He is the promised seed of the woman, who would crush Satan's head – but at the cost of being wounded Himself in the process (Genesis 3:15). In the prophetic writing of David in Psalm 40:6–8, as quoted in Hebrews 10:5–7, it is declared of Jesus that "a [human] body You have prepared for Me. … Then I said, 'Behold, I have come – In the volume of the book it is written of Me – To do Your will, O God'" (NKJV).

THE GREAT HIGH PRIEST

Let us digress briefly to consider the nature of Jesus' office as Great High Priest. We have seen already the function of Aaron, and his successors as high priests of the Levitical priesthood, in the calling to stand in the gap before God as intercessors for the whole nation of Israel, making blood sacrifices to cover over the sin of God's people. Yet these activities being carried out by fallen men could never be more than temporary and inadequate.

Although God has never abolished the Levitical priesthood (Jeremiah 33:17–22), yet for the purpose of achieving the eternal sacrifice which would make possible everlasting atonement and salvation, perfection was required, and an eternal high priest. The messianic prophecy of Psalm 110:4 describes Jesus as "a priest for ever, in the order of Melchizedek". Melchizedek, the enigmatic figure of Genesis 14:18–20 to whom Abraham offered worship by giving a tithe, describes the high priestly role of Jesus in every respect: He was human, He was both a king of peace (Salem) and a priest of the Most High God, His life had no recorded beginning or end, and He was not appointed by men or through generational inheritance.

Nevertheless, despite these essential differences between the priesthood of Melchizedek and Aaron, it remains the case that the work which Jesus accomplished was entirely in accordance with the pattern of the work of Aaron and his successors; they and their sacrifices were the "shadow" (Hebrews 8:5) of which Messiah was to be the substance.

IDENTIFICATION: THE COST TO THE GREAT HIGH PRIEST

We have seen in the example of Aaron and of Esther that true intercession is not simply a matter of words; indeed there are times when no words are needed at all. It is a matter of identification before God with those who are in need of divine intervention.

Jesus' entire life, from His conception in Mary's womb until the morning of His resurrection, was one of constant identification with the pain and difficulty experienced by us, the entire race of human beings who live under the consequences of inherited sin in a fallen world which is groaning in travail. He endured every kind of experience which we encounter in our pain and struggle during our time on earth in our mortal bodies (Hebrews 4:15).

It is astonishing and utterly wonderful that God Himself, in the person of Jesus, should have been willing to become fully human – God in a mortal body, still divine but having deliberately laid aside all His divine advantages (Philippians 2:6–8). What a staggering risk God took for us. We read in Hebrews 4:15 that Jesus experienced every kind of testing and temptation (Greek *peirasmos* has both meanings) that we do; yet without ever responding in a way which was sinful. We take this for granted as being the truth, yet without considering the staggering implications. It is utterly amazing that Jesus lived His entire life on earth as a fully normal human being with every natural instinct and emotion, yet never once sinned by stepping outside the perfection of the will of His Father.

Let us not be deceived: Jesus had no special advantage, no "secret" of immunity against falling into sin, except that of having been born without the inheritance of a sinful nature from His human parents. Because of His divine conception by the Holy Spirit who implanted His body in Mary's womb, He did not have our innate tendency towards rebellion. Yet as the "last [second] Adam" (see 1 Corinthians 15:45), He had to live through every situation in His life exercising His will as a human being in order to obey the will of His Father and not the subtle suggestions of Satan. Had this not been so, the temptations/testings in the wilderness, for example, would have been utterly meaningless; but the fact is that Jesus, like Adam, had the potential to respond in a way which would have been against the Father's will – and had He done so, He would Himself have become a transgressor; His ability to become our Great High Priest would have been lost, and so would our salvation.

THE COST OF OBEDIENCE TO THE WILL OF THE FATHER

"He was despised and rejected by men, a man of sorrows, and familiar with suffering … he took up our infirmities and carried our sorrows … He was oppressed and afflicted … cut off from the land of the living … stricken ….numbered with the transgressors … bore the sin of many …" (Isaiah 53:3–4, 7–8, 12)

The cost of both identifying with us in our human condition, and at the same time living without sin in total submission to the will of the Father, was a lifetime of continual struggle and confrontation, rejection, misunderstanding, scorn and humiliation; it was pain all the way, and demanded constant vigilance against a deadly enemy, the "accuser" (Revelation 12:10) and the "father of lies" (John 8:44), who sought to hinder and ambush Jesus, both directly and through evil-hearted human beings, at every step.

Time and space does not permit us to examine every such instance, but we do not need to do so; we need only to allow the Holy Spirit to use our imaginations and our own experiences to realise the nature of Jesus' intercessory life which has saved us and given us a Great High Priest who permanently represents us before the Father.

The intensity of rejection and suffering must have begun even in Mary's womb. Jesus was being carried in pregnancy by a young woman who would inevitably have been regarded with contempt, and rejected as being immoral. She must have endured agonies of heart and mind, and could have been at risk of being stoned in accordance with the law of Deuteronomy 22:20–21, 23–24. There is no indication that anyone other than Joseph and her cousin Elizabeth believed the incredible truth that she was pregnant by the Holy Spirit. Her friends and family would have scorned and disowned her, and the baby in her womb would have experienced those months of despising and rejection with her.

Nor did the stigma of supposed illegitimacy end at birth. It was used as a weapon of accusation and ridicule against Jesus throughout His life and ministry by those who wished to mock and discredit Him (see e.g. John 8:48; 9:29).

The pain of rejection and betrayal was a permanent feature of Jesus' earthly life. "He came to that which was his own, but his own did not receive him" (John 1:11). It does not take great imagination to realise how difficult His childhood, though unrecorded, must have been. Do we imagine that popularity and acceptance were His experience? He would have been regarded as Mary's illegitimate child, and by His own peers as an extraordinary companion who never broke the rules, while they indulged in the usual childhood traits of malice, rebellion, lies and disobedience. They probably hated Him for His perfection, and His lot would have been loneliness and grief.

Many followed Jesus in the time of His ministry, captivated by the signs and wonders and by the beauty of His teaching; but when He had to speak things which were unpopular or hard to understand, He had to endure the pain of seeing His followers abandon Him (John 6:60–66).

Yet however many or few believed that He was indeed the Messiah, His deadly enemy, Satan, never doubted it. Jesus was pursued by him from the beginning, and His life was always threatened; as an infant in Bethlehem, by Herod's soldiers (Matthew 2:13–18); in His hometown of Nazareth, by an enraged mob who wanted to throw Him off the cliff to His death (Luke 4:23–30).

THE HOUR HAS COME

Finally, at the time of celebration of the Feast of the Passover, came the climax of thirty-three years of unyielding obedience and of consequent anguish which were the pivotal point of all human history. The arrival of certain Greeks was the sign which warned Jesus that His hour of greatest trial was imminent (John 12:20–24). The Great High Priest was not about to finish His earthly ordeal in recognition and acceptance. He knew exactly what lay ahead of Him (John 18:4): betrayal, the most painful form of rejection; a struggle for physical survival in Gethsemane; false accusations; three illegal trials; a Roman scourging; crucifixion and mockery. Through all of this, He had also to carry the agony of knowing the consequences which would fall upon Jerusalem and His Jewish people (Luke 19:41–44; 23:27–31).

At the end, the eternal intercessor, our Great High Priest, endured the greatest agony of identification with the fallen human race; He tasted eternal death in the experience of being separated from His Father, the ultimate pain and terror of abandonment: "My God, my God, why have you forsaken me" (Mark 15:33–34).

That cry of the Great High Priest echoes down the ages. It was the cry of the moment of our salvation, the climax of a life poured out in intercession for a fallen world. He had drunk the cup of sorrows to the very dregs. Then, at last, came the cry of triumph, of complete and eternal victory: "It is finished" (John 19:30).

Therefore, as we ourselves are called to intercede in the demanding times ahead, "Let us fix our eyes on Jesus … who for the joy set before him endured the cross, scorning its shame, and sat down at the right hand of the throne of God" (Hebrews 12:2). He died and is alive for ever more, having the keys of death and Hades (Revelation 1:18) and stands with us in the battle, always making intercession for us with His Father.

QUESTIONS

1. Exodus 17:8–13 contains the account of Joshua's battle against

the Amalekites, in which he prevailed when Moses' hands
held up the staff of God's authority on the hill above, but was
forced back when Moses' hands were lowered through fatigue.
Do you see in this account a clear statement of the principle
that intercession is a vital ingredient of successful spiritual
warfare, without which the front line troops cannot succeed
in their task?

2. The depth of identification often required of an intercessor
can be very costly. Do you think that to be an effective
intercessor requires a special calling from the Lord? If so, what
would you say are the particular qualities needed?

3. Should intercession be corporate in order to have maximum
effect? Can you find both individual and corporate examples
of prevailing intercessory prayer in Scripture?

4. How would you respond if God were to call you to a ministry
of intercession in which the principle emphasis was not on
audible pleadings in prayer, but on the living of a daily life of
costly identification with those for whom you were called to
intercede? Would you be willing to follow in the footsteps of
the Lord Jesus in this way?

ABOUT ISSACHAR
MINISTRIES

Issachar Ministries is named after the tribe of Issachar who in the time of King David was renowned for having men of prayer who *"understood the times and knew what Israel should do"* (1 Chronicles 12.32). The objective of the Ministry, which is based at Moggerhanger Park, Bedfordshire, is to seek understanding, from a Biblical perspective, of current events both in Britain and on the international scene.

The Ministry aims to produce resources which help believers, especially leaders, to understand the times in which we live so that the unchanging Word of God may be more effective in equipping God's people to meet the challenge of presenting the gospel in a secular environment. If the church is to be the prophet to the nation these resources may play a significant part in preparing the way of the Lord.

Dynamic Prayer is an important part of the resources available today which help to overcome the spiritual inertia generated by the pressures of an increasingly secularised society which is *"ever hearing but never understanding; ever seeing but never perceiving"* (Isaiah 6.10).

www.issacharministries.co.uk

About the Author

David Noakes read Law at Pembroke College, Oxford, and practised as a solicitor until called into full-time ministry in 1975.

From 1985 until 1991 he served in ministry with Clifford Hill, becoming leader of the PWM ministry team and subsequently a Trustee of Prophetic Word Ministries. He was for a number of years a visiting teacher for Ellel Ministries and he is a member of Love Never Fails, a group of ministries working together to express love and support and to uphold Biblical truth concerning the Jewish nation. He is also an Advisory Board member of the European Coalition for Israel, which is working in the European Parliament to support the nation of Israel and to declare the Word of God concerning His people, the descendants of Jacob.

For many years he was a member and Elder of Marlow Christian Fellowship, but is now based in South Dorset and commits his time to an itinerant teaching ministry, which has as its chief emphases God's purposes for the nation of Israel, together with the need for preparation and strengthening of the Church for the days to come. He is a Trustee and was until recently Chairman of the Board of Hatikvah Film Trust, a ministry whose principal purpose is to produce film documentaries designed to make known Biblical truth in order to enlighten and to inspire prayer in the Church concerning the Jewish people and the Land of Israel.

He is the author of "The Biblical Basis of Intercession"; a co-author of "Blessing the Church?", a study of the development of the Charismatic Renewal movement; and also a co-author of a book "Israel, His People, His Land, his Story" published by the Love Never Fails group of ministries. This is a Biblically-based refutation of the false teachings of Replacement Theology.

He has been married for 44 years to Valerie, and they have three adult married children and five grandchildren.

We hope you enjoyed reading this
Sovereign World book.
For more details of other Sovereign
books and new releases see our website:

www.sovereignworld.com

Find us on Twitter @sovereignworld

Our authors welcome your feedback on their books.
Please send your comments to our offices.
You can request to subscribe to
our email and mailing list online or by writing to:

**Sovereign World Ltd, PO Box 784,
Ellel, Lancaster, LA1 9DA, United Kingdom
info@sovereignworld.com**

Sovereign World titles are available from
all good Christian bookshops and eBook vendors.

For information about our distributors in the UK,
USA, Canada, South Africa, Australia and Singapore, visit:
www.sovereignworld.com/trade

If you would like to help us send a copy of this book and
many other titles to needy pastors in developing countries,
please write for further information or send your gift to:

Sovereign World Trust, PO Box 777,
Tonbridge, Kent TN11 0ZS
United Kingdom
www.sovereignworldtrust.org.uk
The Sovereign World Trust is a registered charity